Red Light Says Stop!

RED LIGHT

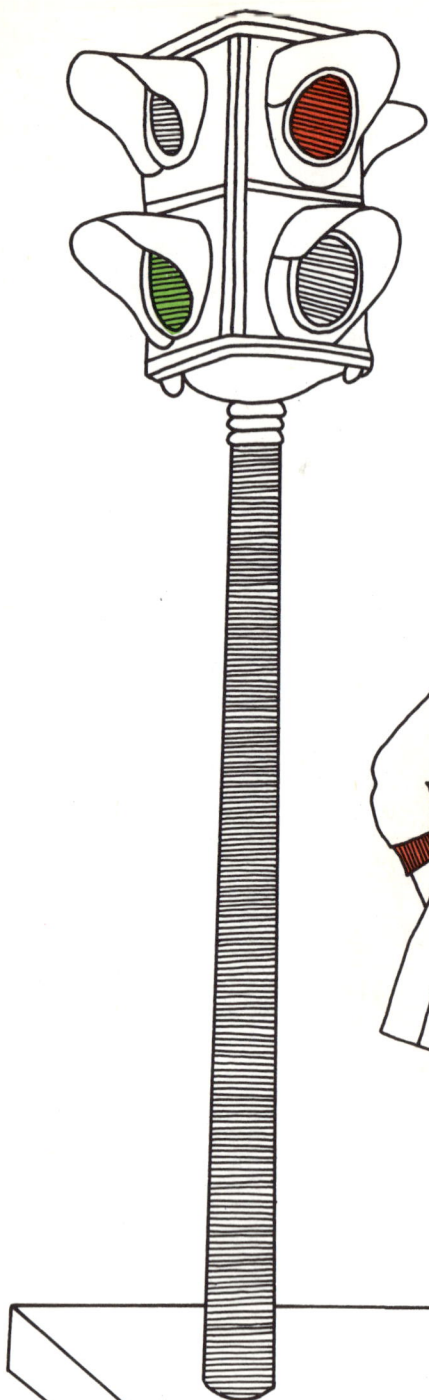

Barbara Rinkoff

SAYS STOP!

illustrated by
Judith Hoffman Corwin

Lothrop, Lee & Shepard Co. • New York

Library of Congress Cataloging in Publication Data

Rinkoff, Barbara.
  Red light says stop!
  SUMMARY: Discusses ways people communicate without talking, such as body
language, Morse code, maps, smoke signals, and pantomime.
    1. Communication—Juvenile literature.   2. Signs and symbols—Juvenile
literature.   1. Communication.   2. Signs and symbols.   I. Corwin,
Judith Hoffman, illus.   II. Title.
P91.R54   001.5′6   74-737
ISBN 0-688-41588-1
ISBN 0-688-51588-6 (lib. bdg.)

Other good books by Barbara Rinkoff

Guess What Grasses Do
Illustrated by Beatrice Darwin

Guess What Trees Do
Illustrated by Beatrice Darwin

To Larry Gurin
a very dear friend who knows how
to communicate

How do people tell things to one another?
What other ways besides talking
can they use to share ideas . . .
show feelings . . .
and sometimes, without even knowing it,
give clues to what they are thinking —
all without saying a word?

You tell things without talking every day.
When you shake your head up and down
you say, YES.

When you shrug your shoulders
you say, I DON'T KNOW.

When you hold your nose with your fingers
you say, IT SMELLS BAD.

Sometimes you tell things without talking
and don't even know it!
This is called using "body language."
When you bite your nails
you say, I'M NERVOUS.

When you wiggle around on your chair
you say, I'M RESTLESS.

When you slam the door
you say, I'M ANGRY.

When you scratch behind your ear
you say, WELL, I DON'T KNOW.

When you smile you say, I'M HAPPY.

Of course, you know how to write.
You put letters together to form words
that tell things.
Newspapers, magazines, this very book —
all use that way of telling things
without speech.

Suppose you wanted to send a secret message
that strangers could not understand.
Instead of writing it in words,
you could use a code.
Let numbers stand for letters,
or one letter stand for another,
or spell all the words backward.

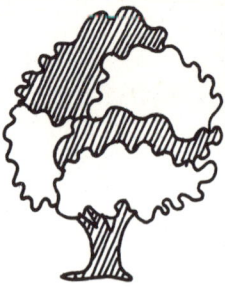

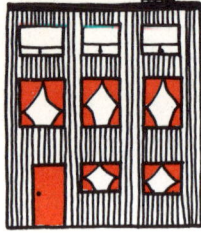

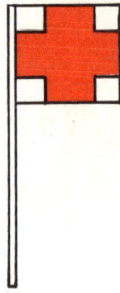

Words are not the only way
to tell things on paper.
A map will tell you many things.
When you travel
you don't even need to ask directions.
Your map will tell you which direction is
North — South — East — or West.
It tells you what roads to use
to go from one place to another.

The pictures on a map tell you things too.

     means railroad tracks

     shows a lake

     is a hospital

Every day we use sounds
to tell things without talking.
Ring your bicycle bell
and you say, WATCH OUT!

The policeman's whistle says, STOP!

In small towns
the blasts of the fire horn
tell volunteer firemen where the fire is.

Ships sound their foghorns in bad weather —
when there is mist, fog, falling snow or rain —
to warn other ships to stay out of their way.

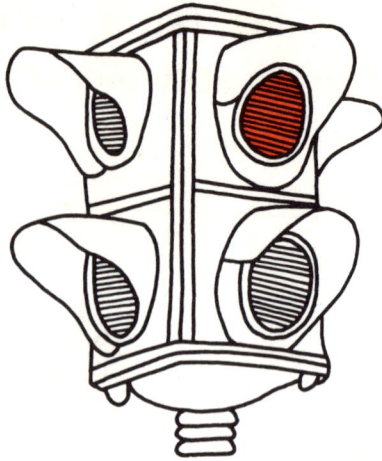

Another way to tell things without talking
is by using lights.
A red traffic light tells drivers, STOP.

And a green traffic light tells drivers, GO.

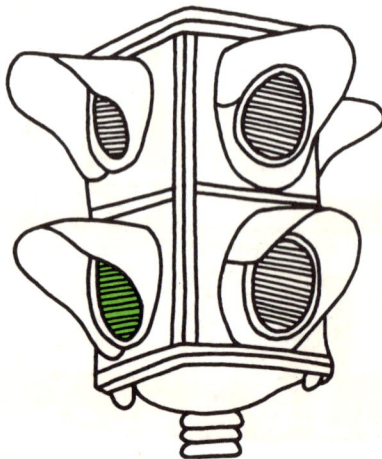

You can make your car lights
tell other drivers
what your car is going to do.
Push the signal left
and your blinking light means, LEFT TURN.

Push the signal right
and your blinking light means, RIGHT TURN.
And you don't have to say a word.

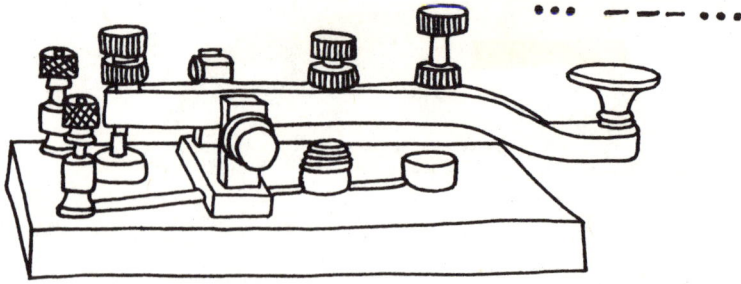

Scouts learn to use the Morse code
to talk with.
They tap out dots, dashes, and spaces
for letters of the alphabet.

A dot is a short buzz.
A dash is a long buzz—
about three times as long as a dot.

With your friend next door you can rig up
a telegraph between your houses
and talk to each other by Morse code.

Or you can send the signals in code.
by turning your flashlight on and off.

Sailors learn the semaphore alphabet
for sending messages.
Hand flags spell out the message.
Each flag position stands for
a letter of the alphabet.

L I O N

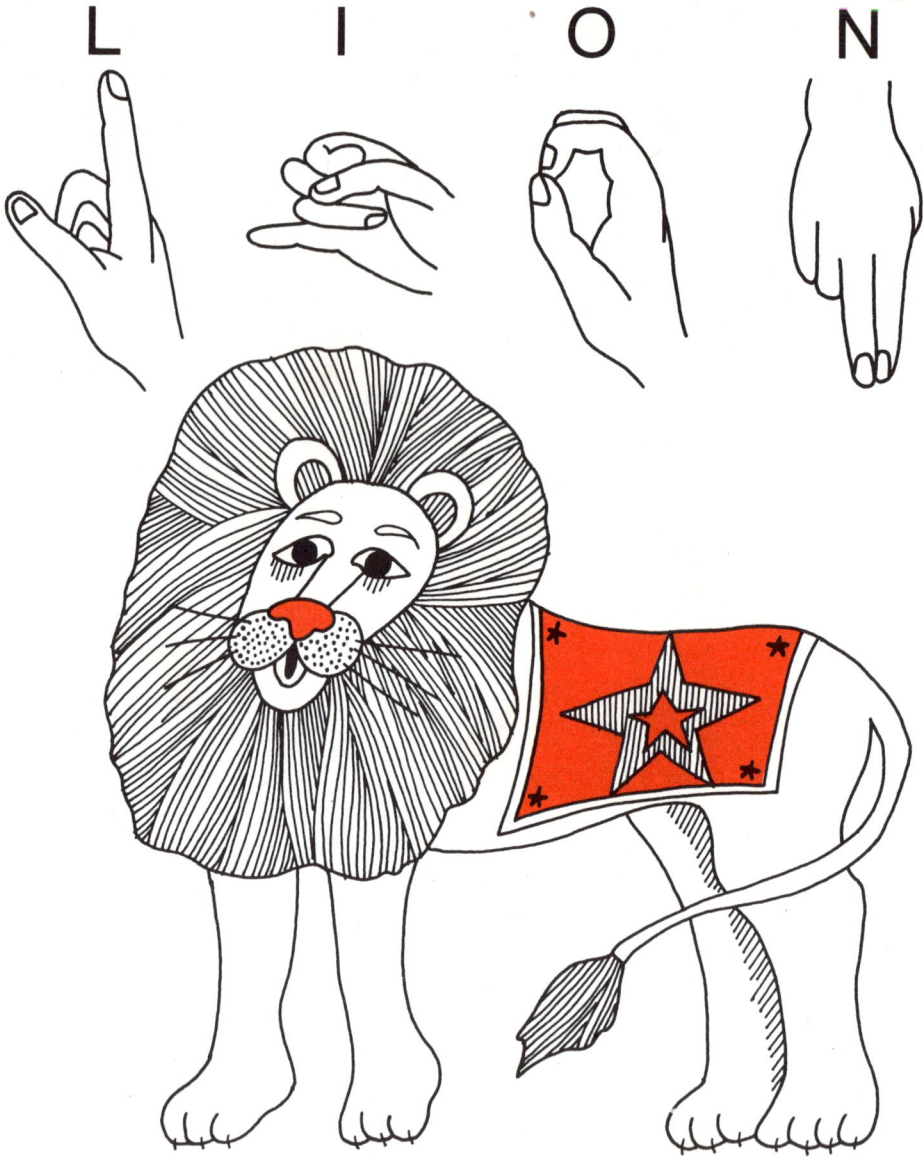

Deaf and dumb people use a different way
to talk to each other.
They use their fingers
to tell things by sign language.

People who cannot see
can be told things in a special way.
Instead of reading letters,
they learn to feel a series
of raised dots on paper—called braille.
Each pattern of dots
stands for a letter of the alphabet.
So a blind person can feel with his fingers
the raised dots on a paper to find out
what the person who wrote the information
wants to tell him.

Thousands of years ago,
when people lived in caves,
they grunted and pointed
to tell things to one another.
Even before there was a spoken language,
or written words,
they learned to draw pictures in the dirt
to tell where to hunt for food,
or to warn that enemies were coming.

The Incas of ancient Peru
used a knotted cord called a quipu
to tell important information.
The knots in the quipu had special meanings.
They could tell the number of animals
or the amount of grain a farmer had
and make a record of
how much gold he owed the king.

American Indians learned to send messages
across distances with smoke signals.

In African jungles,
men found that they could send messages
across the miles to other tribes
by beating drums.

And in one of the Canary Islands,
where there are high mountains
between villages,
shouted words can't be heard
across the distances.
People learned that the sound of whistling
would carry from one mountain
to the next.
So they sent messages to each other
from mountain to mountain by whistling.

Ancient Egyptians
learned to make complicated pictures
called hieroglyphics—
pictures that made up a word or an idea—
so they could share their thoughts
without speaking.
This was one of the first written languages.

CHARIOT

Today each country has its own language
to speak and write.
People who understand the language
can tell things to one another,
but someone who does not know the language
cannot understand.
And so an international symbol language
has been worked out.
Pictures are used to tell the message.
Travelers in foreign lands
can read these picture signs,
which mean the same thing in all languages.

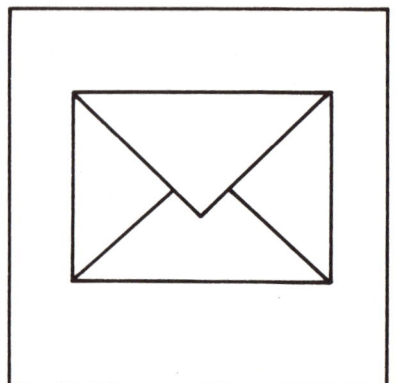

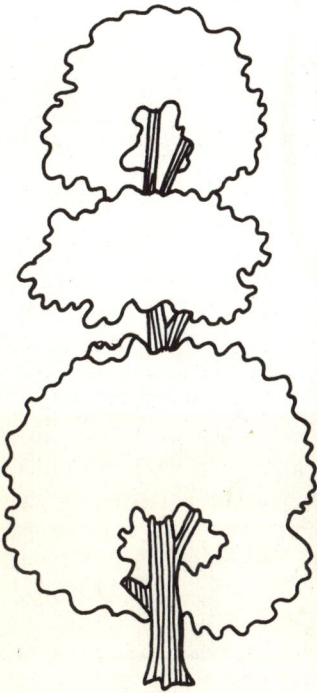

For example, a picture on a street corner
of a man walking means, CROSS STREET HERE.
A picture of a triangle
with an old-fashioned train in it
means, RAILROAD CROSSING.

Trying to act out ideas without talking
can be fun too.
It is called pantomime.
Instead of the voice, the thought is told
with the face, hands, and body.
You can tell a whole story in pantomime
without speaking a word.
If you are "it" in the game of charades,
you must not talk.
You must use pantomime
to act out a word or phrase
that the other players try to guess.

It is easy to see that there are many ways
to tell things without talking.
You could try some by yourself.
You could draw a map showing the way
from your school to your house.
You could act out a story in pantomime.
You could write a letter to a friend in code.

Can you think of still other ways
to share ideas without speaking?

DATE DUE			
DEC 10 76			
DEC 18 79			
MAY 2 77			